For Sarah Helen Meisel Stone,
my beloved grandmother,
who showed us all what a strong woman was,
every day of her life
—T. L. S.

For Felix

—R. G.

Henry Holt and Company, LLC
Publishers since 1866
175 Fifth Avenue
New York, New York 10010
www.HenryHoltKids.com

Henry Holt® is a registered trademark of Henry Holt and Company, LLC.
Text copyright © 2008 by Tanya Lee Stone
Illustrations copyright © 2008 by Rebecca Gibbon
All rights reserved.
Distributed in Canada by H. B. Fenn and Company Ltd.

Photo of Elizabeth Cady Stanton (facing page): L. Tom Perry Special Collections,
Harold B. Lee Library, Brigham Young University, Provo, Utah

Library of Congress Cataloging-in-Publication Data
Stone, Tanya Lee.
Elizabeth leads the way : Elizabeth Cady Stanton and the right to vote / Tanya Lee Stone ;
illustrations by Rebecca Gibbon.—1st ed.
p.   cm.
ISBN-13: 978-0-8050-7903-6
ISBN-10: 0-8050-7903-3
1. Stanton, Elizabeth Cady, 1815–1902—Juvenile literature.   2. Suffragists—United States—
Biography—Juvenile literature.   3. Social reformers—United States—Biography—
Juvenile literature.   I. Gibbon, Rebecca.   II. Title.
HQ1413.S67S76 2008   305.42092—dc22 [B]   2007002833

First Edition—2008 / Designed by Barbara Grzeslo
The artist used gouache and color pencils on paper to create the illustrations for this book.
Printed in China on acid-free paper. ∞

1 3 5 7 9 10 8 6 4 2

*"We do not expect our path will be strewn
with the flowers of popular applause,
but over the thorns of bigotry and prejudice
will be our way."*

—ELIZABETH CADY STANTON

Elizabeth lady Stanton

What would you do
if someone told you
you can't be what you want to be
because you are a girl?

What would you do
if someone told you
your vote doesn't count,
your voice doesn't matter
because you are a girl?

Would you ask why?
Would you talk back?
Would you fight . . .
for your rights?

Elizabeth did.

All of these things used to be true
back when Elizabeth Cady was a girl.

And all of these things might still be true today
if Elizabeth hadn't led the way.

She was only four years old the first time she heard
someone, a *woman*, say life was better for boys.

The woman had come to visit Elizabeth's new baby sister.
"What a pity it is she's a girl!"

How could anyone look at a little baby and feel sad?
What could be wrong about being a girl?

She was thirteen years old
when her father, Judge Cady,
told a woman whose husband had died
that the farm she had spent her whole life working on
would be taken from her.
Without a husband, the law stated,
nothing belonged to her.

Elizabeth was horrified by this unfairness.
She said that the law should be cut out of every book!

Judge Cady told her that wouldn't
change anything.
The law was still the law.
And only men were allowed to change laws.

PrePOSterous!

She decided
right then and there
that she could do anything
any boy could do.

She jumped over high hurdles on horseback.

She rafted across a raging river.

She won a prize for being the best in Greek studies.

Her father was proud.
But he worried about his strong-spirited,
rule-breaking daughter.

"Ah, you should have been a boy!"
He knew how much easier
her life would be.
But Elizabeth wasn't interested in easy.

At sixteen, since colleges would not let girls in,
Elizabeth begged her father to send her
to a girls' school to continue her learning.

So, while most young ladies were
getting married,
washing dishes,

doing laundry,

and having babies,

Elizabeth was studying religion, math,
science, French, and writing.

Several years later, Elizabeth Cady
met Henry Stanton.

He was an abolitionist,
speaking out against slavery.

He understood how unfair it was for people
not to have rights or power.

He did not laugh
when Elizabeth talked
about freedom.

He did not laugh
when Elizabeth said all people
should be able to live life
the way *they* chose.

And he did not laugh
when she told him
she would add his name to her own
but would not give up hers
just to marry him.

So Elizabeth Cady
became Elizabeth Cady Stanton and
had babies, cooked meals, washed dishes,
mended clothes, and did laundry.

She loved her babies, but she did *not* love
cooking and dishes and mending and laundry.

One day her friend Lucretia Mott invited her to a lunch.

Lucretia had always shared Elizabeth's ideas
about all the things women could do, and would do,
if only they had the right.
The other women at lunch shared them, too.

Elizabeth got fired up. She proposed they hold a meeting.

A meeting that would gather together
lots and lots of women
from all around to talk.

But what would they talk about?

There were so *many* things
that needed to be set straight.

Married women
couldn't own property
or even the money
they worked to earn!

Elizabeth had learned long ago
that only men could change the laws.

Because only men could vote.

That was **it!**

That was the *one* thing
that could change *every*thing.

If women could vote,
they could help change
all kinds of laws!

This idea was so shocking,
so huge,
so daring—
Elizabeth's friends gasped out loud!

If they were flabbergasted,
what would other people think?

Elizabeth did not waver.
She knew voting was the only way
to make a difference.

Her battle cry for the right to vote rang out:
"Have it, we must. Use it, we will."

Even her Henry thought she had gone too far.

But on July 19, 1848,
when Elizabeth arrived at the meeting place,
she saw for herself that she hadn't.

The small church in Seneca Falls, New York,
was filled with hundreds of people.

Elizabeth read aloud
what she and a few of the women
had written together.

Their Declaration of Right and Sentiments
challenged the idea from the Declaration of Independence
that "all *men* are created equal."

When she was finished,
she looked into the faces of the crowd and waited.

The room was silent!
Then a rumbling began.
It grew louder and louder and louder
as people argued whether or not
women should be allowed to vote.

San Francisco

VOTES for WOMEN !

VOTES for WOMEN

VOTES for WOMEN

VOTES for WOMEN

Word of the meeting spread like wildfire.

Newspapers across the country scolded Elizabeth for her boldness.

But other women joined her in battle.

The idea of women having the right to vote began to buzz in the ears of people from Maine to California.

Elizabeth had tossed a stone in the water
and the ripples grew wider and wider and wider.

Many said Elizabeth must be stopped.
But she was unstoppable.
She changed America forever.